PHOTO CREDITS: All photographs by Jack Andrzej Gancarz, with the following exceptions: Historical Society of Palm Beach County; 11, 12, 15, 16, 19, 20, 23, 24, 27, 28, 31, 32, 34, 35. The Breakers; 55 (above), 55 (below), 81. Peggo Cromer; 75 (above). Palm Beach Opera Company; 75 (below). Bill Helfferich; 86 (above). Ed-diee White; 95 (above). Sam Grisso/Mr. "G" photo; 95 (below).

Published by Downtown Photo Service Press
1707 Crestwood Boulevard
Lake Worth, Florida 33460 USA
Telephone (407) 582-4835

Copyright © 1989 Downtown Photo Service Press

ISBN 0-9620260-0-X

Printed in Hong Kong by South China Printing Co.

Palm Beach

☐ FLORIDA'S RIVIERA ☐

PHOTOGRAPHY & TEXT BY JACK ANDRZEJ GANCARZ

(cover) One of Mizner's most beautifully designed mansions contains a spacious second story terrace, an open loggia, and two swimming pools; one for morning use and the other for afternoon bathing. The mansion formally owned by the late John Lennon.

(page 3) Breathtaking sunset over Palm Beach.

(pages 4 - 5) Scenic Ocean Boulevard.

(page 6) Fountain at the entrance to *The Breakers*.

(page 8) Gucci courtyard off *Worth Avenue*.

ACKNOWLEDGEMENTS

I would like to extend my deepest appreciation to my parents, and my brother Nick for their undaunted faith, encouragement and interest in my dream. I would especially like to thank my mother for her aid and support in making that dream come true.

I want to thank the following people who have helped in the preparation of this book: Flora L. Doone; typography and editing. Lillian Reyes; editing. Lizette Rodriguez; editing. Kurt Bretz; layout.

Special thanks to the following people: Lynne and Martin Glatter; Halina and William Kobielski,

The following: Historical Society of Palm Beach County, Henry Morrison Flagler Museum, Royal Poincianna Chapel, Society of the Four Arts Library, Ballet Florida, Palm Beach Opera, United States Croquet Association, The Breakers, and the Brazilian Court Hotel. Also, Mrs. Frank M. McMahon, Joseph F. Dryer Jr. Family, Jackey Perez, Edward A. Lutz III, Nancy Hirsch, Donny Thompson, Terrence Kadyszewski, Ann Frost, Lee Frost, Ross Little, and Gail Sylvester — without whose cooperation this book would not be complete.

Palm Beach. An island of beauty and decadence. Captured here in these pages is an ambience of wealth and splendor which Jack chose to share with us. And why not? Once your eyes have travelled the route of this book a new backdrop of dreams will be created for you — mansions fit for kings, sun drenched beaches and lush landscapes. The history provided will fill you with awe as to how just a few men with grand ideas could turn a piece of land into the grandest "millionaire's playground". To photograph an image is one thing. To convey an idea is another. Jack has successfully conquered both with these images of grandeur.

— Flora L. Doone

Palm Beach probably would not have been transformed into a premier winter resort had it not been for the misfortune of a Spanish sailing vessel, the *Providencia.* Enroute to Cadiz, Spain from the Caribbean island of Trinidad, the vessel met her peril on Florida's treacherous coast during a tropical storm. The ship, along with its precious cargo of coconuts, was swept ashore on Palm Beach on January 9, 1878. Two clever homesteaders living near-by, claimed the estimated 20,000 coconuts and began selling them to other settlers for two-and-a-half cents apiece. The coconuts were then planted along the lake and the beach. Fourteen years later when Henry Morrison Flagler — the mastermind responsible for developing Florida's east coast — visited the area, he found a lush tropical isle drenched with alien coconut palms. The cool ocean breeze, sunny weather, and the pleasant tropical atmosphere appealed to Flagler so much that within three days he decided to build the world's largest resort hotel, *The Royal Poinciana.*

Before transforming Palm Beach into a resort mecca, Flagler's enterprising instinct was captured by St. Augustine, a town 200 miles north of Palm Beach. He first visited there in 1878 with his ailing first wife, Mary Harkness Flagler, hoping that Florida's balmy climate would comfort her. Mary's health continued to deteriorate and she eventually passed away. In the years that followed, Flagler withdrew from his corporate position in The Standard Oil Company to pursue his interests in Florida. During this time he fell in love and married Ida Alice Shourds, the woman who had cared for Mary during her illness and consoled Flagler after her death.

□ ■ □

It was while honeymooning in St. Augustine with Ida that Flagler realized the potential of the old historic city as a winter

Mr. and Mrs. Flagler hosting an outdoor social gathering.

resort. But in order to attract the social elite to his intended resort, Flagler knew he had to improve and hasten traveling conditions. While northeasterners had already been making a twenty-nine hour railroad trip from New York City to Jacksonville, Florida, arriving at St. Augustine required a tedious ferry ride across the St. John's River followed by a slow journey by train on a narrow-gauge track. Flagler funded the building of a bridge over the river, bought the narrow-gauge line and converted it to standard gauge. Now the wealthy would be able to travel in their private railroad cars non-stop from New York City to St. Augustine. The railroad had proven its importance in providing an impetus for the further development of Florida's coast.

■ □ ■

Thomas Hastings, a Paris trained architect and his partner John M. Carrere, were commissioned by Flagler to design a hotel reminiscent of Spanish architecture. Flagler envisioned a grand hotel with open courtyards, tropical retreats, fountains, towers, and decor suggestive of St. Augustine's history.

Costing over $2,500,000, the luxurious 540 room *Ponce de Leon* was opened in 1888. Because of its success, Flagler commissioned the same architects to design a second hotel, *The Alcazar*. He later purchased a hotel adjacent to The Alcazar and connected the two.

☐ ■ ☐

While Flagler's exclusive resort hotels drew the rich and prominent to St. Augustine, the marsh lands near present day Palm Beach were settled by adventure seekers, pioneering farmers, and occasional shipwreck victims, as well as any war surviving Seminole Indians. Life was difficult for these early homesteaders who were isolated from "civilization". Farming proved to be frustrating under sub-tropic climates, and the lack of efficient transportation hampered distribution of fruits and vegetables to other states. However, with an abundance of fish, deer, and wild foul inhabiting the area, hunting and fishing became a good source for food.

■ ☐ ■

By the 19th century the Florida lighthouse system had deteriorated, hence passing ships often fell victim to winter storms, summer hurricanes, and dangerous reefs. The settlers salvaged the shipwrecks in order to utilize the wood for building houses. They also used the various cargo to barter for needed staples such as coffee and flour from the nearest general store, located 150 miles up the coast. Fortunately contact with the rest of the state was provided by a postal carrier, whose route began in Palm Beach and ended in the settlement of Miami. Since there were no roads, he walked down the coast, braving mosquitos and occasional alligators. To facilitate his long trek, he walked near the shoreline where the sand is the firmest and took his shoes off to preserve the leather, thus becoming known as the "barefoot mailman".

By the time Flagler came to Palm Beach in 1892, the area was sprawling with little communities, including three small hotels. The first hotel in the area was *The Cocoanut Grove House*. It began when "Cap" Dimick, an early settler, built an

Private railroad cars were conveniently located adjacent to *The Royal Poinciana.*

eight room addition to his house on the lake. He catered to the winter tourists and the sport fishermen. In the off-season it was the center for social gatherings for the local residents. The hotel subsequently boasted fifty rooms. The tropical setting had already attracted several wealthy families who built beautiful winter homes on the lakeside. Their practice of sailing down for the winter season still continues today.

■ □ ■

The late 1800's was the era of industrialization in America and the emergence of business tycoons who gained great wealth and power. Successful men such as Cornelius Vanderbilt, Andrew Carnegie, J.P. Morgan, John D. Rockefeller, and Henry Morrison Flagler earned esteem in the country's discriminating industrial and financial circles. Using his relative's money, Flagler had made his fortune by helping to form The Standard Oil Company with Rockefeller and Samuel Andrews.

□ ■ □

Four o'clock tea was enjoyed in the *Coconut Grove*.

Flagler wasted no time in using his accumulated wealth to achieve his goal of building the biggest resort hotel the world has ever known. He ordered land to be purchased from settlers living in the Palm Beach area. Two parcels on the island stretching from the lakeside to the ocean and two on the mainland were purchased for a total of $170,000. Once the word broke out of Flagler's intentions to build a resort hotel and to extend the railroad down to Palm Beach, property prices skyrocketed prompting the area's first land-boom. The land that pioneers had homesteaded increased in value from $150 an acre to $1000 an acre.

■ □ ■

The ground was broken for The Royal Poinciana Hotel in May of 1893. Thousands of laborers and craftsmen had to be brought into the area from the north and the Bahama islands. They earned $1.50 to $2.25 a day and were housed in tents and shacks in an area just north of the construction site known as the "Styx".

□ ■ □

The 540 room hotel was completed in 1894 in just nine months with additions being built in 1899 and 1901 due to its popularity with the social elite. Eventually it encompassed thrity-two acres and could accomodate 1,750 guests. The six-story hotel had three miles of corridors and its dining room seated 1,600. It was at that time, the largest wooden hotel in the world.

■ □ ■

Skeptics were leary of Flagler's ability to lure so many tourists to an isolated wilderness. But Flagler knew that the success of his hotel in Palm Beach, as in St. Augustine, depended greatly on reliable and convenient transportation. He extended the Florida East Coast Railroad to Palm Beach two months after The Royal Poinciana Hotel's opening. Having built a reputation for colossal hotels with pristine surroundings and impeccable furnishings, Flagler had no difficulty in attracting his clientele to Palm Beach.

□ ■ □

By extending his railroad down Florida's east coast, building impressive hotels, and creating lavish resorts, Flagler was realizing his dream of an "American Riviera". At the time, the only other sea-side resorts with a favorable winter climate were the French and Italian Rivieras. At the time, travel to Europe by steamship was hazardous, time consuming, and more expensive, than traveling to Florida. Besides, according to Flagler, "Europe is a place where people come from. Nobody should actually *go* there."

■ □ ■

The wealthy and prominent were satisfied coming to Palm Beach, and why not? The Royal Poinciana offered all the

amenities one could ask for, as long as money was no object. A double room with bath could be had for $38 a day and a 10 room suite for $100, an exorbitant amount those days. The hotel's architecture resembled the Georgian style. Tall Corinthian columned verandas lined with rows of rocking chairs overlooked the tropically landscaped grounds. A number of parlors and a magnificent ballroom were accessible to guests. Afternoon tea was held in the tea garden, appropriately named the *Coconut Grove*, for its numerous coconut palms. Served with tea was none other than fresh "coconut" cake. Musical entertainment was provided by a nationally known orchestra each weekday afternoon.

□ ■ □

The hotel's exterior was painted a vivid yellow, which came

The Royal Poinciana Hotel, at the time the largest wooden resort hotel in the world.

to be known as "Flagler yellow", and the shutters green. The interior walls were covered with green and white patterned paper, and the floors with a thick green Japanese matting. Every room had a gold-trimmed white porcelain chamberpot adorned inside and out with green palm trees, discretely concealed in the night stand, of course.

■ ☐ ■

Two years after the hotel's opening, Flagler had a railroad bridge built over Lake Worth to Palm Beach so that resorters could have their private railroad cars conveniently adjacent to the hotel and forego the usual ferry ride across the lake. In addition to shortening the distance, the wealthy could easily call on their personal servants who remained in the cars throughout the stay.

☐ ■ ☐

Paradise would not be complete until the Styx, situated adjacent to The Royal Poinciana, had been moved off the island resort. The workers however, had no intentions of moving at Flagler's request, even though he promised them land for homestead. Being a keen businessman, Flagler was not about to have his investment in Palm Beach jeopardized. He scheduled a circus to be held across the lake in celebration of the hotel's completion. While all the laborers were enjoying themselves in West Palm Beach, their belongings were gathered up and their tents and shacks burned down. The next morning they were hustling about, claiming the surveyed land in West Palm Beach for their new homes.

■ □ ■

Despite his ambition to develop his newly found paradise, Flagler's generousity never ceased. He donated a water plant, an electric generator, a telephone switchboard and even a fire truck equipped with a hand-operated pump to serve West Palm Beach and his resort. He also contributed to local churches, regardless of denomination. Flagler wanted to establish a permanent residence for the laborers. He knew that without employees living near-by to attend to the needs of his discriminating clientel, Palm Beach would not have become the country's most fashionable winter gathering spot.

□ ■ □

Due to the enormous popularity of The Royal Poinciana Hotel, Flagler built a wooden oceanfront hotel, *The Palm Beach Inn*, in 1896. Less formal and less pretentious than The Royal Poinciana, it attracted a younger set. Additions were added and it was renamed *The Breakers*. In 1903 fire had destroyed the structure completely, but Flagler immediately ordered a new one to be built on a larger scale. Adjacent to the hotel on both sides, Flagler had built wooden framed and shingled cottages for his more prominent guests and friends who preferred not to reside in the hotel. Wintering in these cottages were families of such notable men as John D. Rockefeller, J. P. Morgan, John Jacob Astor, William Randolph Hearst, and President Warren C. Harding. Of these cottages, only three remain.

The *Lazy-Backs,* a popular form of transportation in Palm Beach.

■ □ ■

The Breakers' casino pool and the "sands", as the beach was known, even attracted the guests from The Royal Poinciana. It was a standing custom to be at the sands before noon. Formal attire was considered the *social norm* of the time. Men were garbed in suits and the women in long dresses. Those who ventured into the ocean were required to abide by the strict rules imposed by The Breakers. These rules dictated that women were to wear long black stockings preventing the exposure of any flesh. A mule-drawn trolley transported beach goers from Lake Worth to The Breakers. The only other means of transportation allowed on the island by Flagler were bicycles and "lazy-backs". These were converted tricycles, with rik-shaw type wicker chairs in front and pedalled by a driver from the rear, so as not to obstruct the picturesque view of the sightseer.

□ ■ □

At about this time, Flagler's second wife Ida Alice began

It was customary for *everyone* to be at the beach by noon.

having delusions and even claimed to have communicated through a *Ouija board* with the Czar of Russia. Flagler spared no expense on medical treatments. However, without any improvement in her condition, the courts ruled her insane and she was committed to an asylum for mental illness. She was well cared for until she died in 1930.

□ ■ □

Using his clout, Flagler persuaded Florida's legislators to pass a law making divorce on the grounds of insanity possible. He divorced Ida and announced his engagement to Mary Lily Kenan, marrying her three days later in 1901. Flagler was now 71, and Mary, 34 years old. They had met ten years earlier in St. Augustine at The Ponce de Leon Hotel and had kept in contact throughout the years. She told Flagler that she wanted to live in a "marble mansion". As a wedding gift, Flagler commissioned the same two architects who designed The Ponce de Leon Hotel to design it. Construction of *Whitehall* had begun even before the wedding. It cost over $2,500,000 to build, another $1,500,000 in furnishings and required importing most of the paintings and sculptures from Europe. In effect, it was a white marble palace with rooms imitating styles of European nobility. This truly remarkable display of grandeur was a setting for magnificent and elegant galas.

■ □ ■

To further the progress of Palm Beach, as "America's Riviera", Flagler persuaded an old business associate, E.R. Bradley, to join him in his efforts. It was Flagler who first encouraged Bradley to open a Monte Carlo style casino in St. Augustine. Flagler believed that the same success could be achieved in Palm Beach. Bradley, along with Flagler envisioned Palm Beach as the "millionaire's playground of America".

□ ■ □

His ambition was to open the most exclusive, the most discriminating, and the most expensive club in the world. When the "Beach Club", as it was named, opened for the winter season in 1899, women were not allowed to participate in gambling. Before the end of the season the club was due to close its doors. The expected success was never realized. On the eve before the closing, E.R. Bradley's brother John decided to allow women to try their luck at gambling for the first time in any American casino. Needless to say, that night was a venerable success and the club went on to enjoy fifty more profitable years. It was proclaimed comparable, if not superior, to the casinos of Monte Carlo.

■ □ ■

Even though gambling was illegal in the state of Florida, Bradley was able to operate his casino. Membership in the club was exclusive to winter resorters, year-round residents were not permitted in the club. Because of this discrimination, he convinced the legislature that his establishment was attracting much needed revenue to the state. The gambling laws were never enforced upon the "Beach Club".

□ ■ □

E.R. Bradley's *Beach Club*, was a Monte Carlo style casino.

Because of the success of his club, Bradley became second only to Flagler as a catalyst in the development of Palm Beach. He enticed northerners by convincing them that moving to Florida would add twenty years to their life span. Bradley was a shrewd businessman. Not only was he strict with his help, but he also set very high standards for his members. Proper attire and decorum were expected at all times. Besides a gambling interest, Bradley was also very fond of horses. His Kentucky farm produced four Kentucky Derby winners. He went on to use his profits from purse-winnings and gambling revenues to make donations to various local charities.

■ ☐ ■

While The Breakers and The Royal Poinciana offered dining, entertainment, shopping and transportation for their patrons, Bradley's Beach Club became the only alternative that Flagler allowed in Palm Beach. Shortly following Flagler's death in 1913 and during the World War I years, the hotels began to lose their dominance on social life. This change

Alligator Joe and his hunting expedition.

began with the opening of The Fifth Avenue Shops on Main Street, now known as Royal Poinciana Way. The pattern of social life continued to change with the founding of *The Everglades Club*, as it became the center for social gatherings.

□ ■ □

It was originally intended as a convalescents' club for American war victims, but due to lack of interest it was converted into a private club by Paris Singer, of the sewing machine family. He had commissioned an architect who would change the look of Palm Beach with his unique Mediterranean-Revival style; a man by the name of Addison Mizner. The Everglades Club was designed in a collage of Mediterranean architectural styles. It had lovely porticos, an expansive courtyard, and a California mission style tower. The interior was laid in colorful Spanish and North African tiles and furnished with antiques. The diverse style was described by an observer as a "Bastard-Spanish-Moorish-Romanesque-Rennaisance-Bull-Market-Damn-The-Expense style!" It was easy to understand how this extraordinary display of eclectic architectural splendor swayed Singer from philanthropic intentions to capitalistic ones rather quickly.

■ □ ■

Paris Singer met Mizner in New York after fleeing war-torn Europe. Mizner, who was recuperating from an injury, was delighted to have been invited to spend the winter in Palm Beach with Singer. Since the new home market was soft due to the war, there was little work for him. Singer had purchased land previously occupied by "Alligator Joe" — a favorite tourist attraction during the late nineteenth and early twentieth centuries. He wrestled alligators and sold stuffed baby alligator souvenirs. The Everglades Club was built on this land and the adjacent road became the beginning of the world-famous *Worth Avenue*.

□ ■ □

The Everglades Club became increasingly popular with the

socially prominant. Enterntainment, fine dining, tennis and golf were available to its members. It also provided an informal atmosphere for socializing — a sharp contrast from the strict rule of formality found at the hotels. Singer even introduced Riviera-style clothing to Palm Beach living, thus keeping up with the "American Riviera" image. Evenings at the club, however, still remained formal. Members wore the most fashionable clothing and the ladies donned their most expensive and impressive jewels. Singer was extremely selective in allowing membership to the club. Not only did his policy ostracize the bourgeois but also gave him the power to manipulate the upper-class since annual membership in his club became a criterion for a position in society.

Once again, Singer commissioned Mizner. He was now to develop Worth Avenue by designing buildings with commercial space and residences for club members. In his plans, Mizner included spacious courtyards, fountains and lovely *vias* which gave the Avenue an ambiance of old world

El Mirasol, a Mizner mansion designed for the "Grand Dame" of Palm Beach.

charm. He even designed and located his own apartment and office in Via Mizner, across from The Everglades Club. The shops of distinction quickly relocated to the Avenue, situating themselves near the discriminating and wealthy. The Avenue rose to notable status and achieved international acclaim in the ensuing years.

□ ■ □

Mizner's reputation as a prominant architect rose to new heights when Mrs. Eva Cromwell Statesbury, the "grand dame" of Palm Beach society, first saw the splendor of the Everglades Club. So impressed was Eva Cromwell, that she immediately replaced her Philadelphia architect with Mizner, even though her previous architect's plans for her mansion were complete. Mizner spent one million dollars in building *El Mirasol*. It had

The Everglades Club was originally intended for convalescing war veterans.

thirty-seven rooms, a forty car garage, a stately dining room, impressive courtyards, a living room capable of seating 175 guests, an aviary and a private zoo. This imposing edifice became the site of extensive entertaining. Its entrance contained a lofty flight of stairs where "Queen Eva", as she was called behind her back, would majestically greet her guests wearing one of her haute couture gowns and complementing it with her brilliant jewels. Once society viewed this colossal work of architectural beauty, Mizner became extremely sought after. He went on to design office buildings, clubs and other grand villas in his unique style.

■ □ ■

This Mediterranean-Revival style necessitated the use of materials not readily available. Mizner founded a factory, *Los Manos*, where he produced terra-cotta barrel roof tiles, cut coral stone blocks, wrought iron work, stained and leaded glass windows, stone and wood carvings, and antique-like furniture. Mizner supplemented these with trips to Europe to purchase authentic works.

Mizner was fulfilling his visions of Medieval romance and legend. He insisted on authenticity often using unconventional working methods to create the look he wanted. He had stone staircases chipped at the edges so as to imitate the wear caused by spurs worn by Spanish knights. Carvings on wooden doors were scratched and nicked with chisels. He had marble work cracked with a sledgehammer and then cemented together. Mizner even went as far as whipping furniture with chains in order to appear centuries old.

□ ■ □

Mizner's success coincided with the free-spirited mood of the twenties. The war had brought new prosperity to the nation. American industry changed rapidly with new inventions and innovations which helped to create a materialistic society. What were once considered "luxuries", now became necessities. The Nouveau Riche as well as the Old Guard had plenty to spend and needed a place to spend it. The "winter playground" became their destination. As more resorters arrived in Palm Beach, the season became longer, The

The 1925 *Breaker's* fire left 1,000 guests without lodgings.

wealthy commissioned architects to design ostentatious mansions in the popular Mediterranean-Revival style, thus replacing the modest frame and shingle "Victorian" cottage of the early 1900's.

■　□　■

As Private Clubs became the commonplace for social events and the wealthy turned toward residences, The Royal Poinciana and The Breakers lost their prominence in resort life. In 1925 a fire had devastated The Breakers, and the tragic hurricanes of 1926 and 1928 damaged The Royal Poinciana. The Breakers was rebuilt once again, this time with concrete. It was able to regain its former glory as a world class hotel. By now The Royal Poinciana had become obsolete, unlike the new Breakers. It could not offer guests the *modern* luxury of a private bath in each room. Eventually it was torn down during the Depression. At first Palm Beach living was not profoundly effected by the Stock Market Crash of October, 1929. The extremely wealthy continued hosting extravagant galas. Their attitude, however, began changing in the ensuing years.

Addison Mizner, his friend, Mrs. Singer, and Paris Singer enjoy a relaxing moment.

Flaunting one's wealth was no longer in vogue as the nation desperately struggled to restructure its economy. As *Fortune Magazine* wrote in 1936, "Life in Palm Beach is above all else private: There is little venturing into public places. You entertain in your own home or you tour among the homes of your friends. High walls shelter you from the grim world of the anonymous poor." As the season continued to lengthen, more modest and practical homes were built. Some of the more popular styles at this time included Bermudian, West Indies Colonial, Monterey, and Art Moderne. Some of these more modest homes as well as some of Mizner's mansions were demolished throughout the years. As a result, Palm Beach has developed a new interest in preserving and maintaining its remaining historical landmarks.

□ ■ □

Palm Beach society continues to host elegant galas benefiting charitable organziations. These events have attracted a diverse public, from the Prince and Princess of Wales to Hollywood greats like Elizabeth Taylor and Bob Hope, as well as prominent businessmen such as Donald Trump. Many of today's widely known and esteemed figures make Palm Beach their seasonal as well as year-round home. The world-class hotels and restaurants continue to pamper those with discriminating tastes. Legendary Worth Avenue offers elegant and exclusive shopping from haute couture originals to fabulous jewels. This unique combination has given Palm Beach its international appeal.

■　□　■

(page 37) *The Bath and Tennis Club* was built in 1926 in reaction to Paris Singer's autocratic dominance of the Everglades Club. It is said that this is the site where the "Providencia" had wrecked, spilling its historically significant cargo of coconuts.

Mar-a-Lago, as its name suggests, stretches from the ocean to the lake on 18 acres of prime real estate. It was constructed in the 1920's for the wife of E.F. Hutton, Mrs. Marjorie Merriweather Post — also the daughter of the cereal magnate.

The grandest of Palm Beach mansions, Mar-a-Lago boasts a nine hole golf course, orange grove, tennis court, swimming pool, private beach and 122 lavishly furnished rooms. It is presently owned by real estate tycoon Donald Trump.

A Romanesque loggia separates the tennis court from the swimming pool in this Mediterranean Revival mansion. The three most prominent Palm Beach architects of the 1920's — Addison Mizner, Maurice Fatio and Marion Wyeth — had contributed to its design at various times.

Building imposing and intriguing facades was a common architectural practice of the Mediterranean Revival style. This was designed by the renown architect Marion Wyeth.

Mizner's unique architectural style necessitated the use of various building materials not readily available. He founded a factory which produced, among other things, cut coral stone blocks.

"The Bastard-Spanish-Moorish-Romanesque-Gothic-Renaissance-Bull-Market-Damn-The-Expense-Style" was how Mizner's work was described and owning one of his mansions in the 1920's was a must for the social elite.

Authenticity was Addison Mizner's trademark. He paid particularly close attention to small details, despite the fact that he often improvised from the original blue prints.

This Mizner designed Spanish Colonial Revival mansion served as the winter *Whitehouse* during John F. Kennedy's presidency.

Two Palm Beach homes of Estee Lauder, whose line of cosmetics is one of the country's largest prestige-brands sold in better department stores.

Rolling waves, coconut palms, and homes designed by Mizner, make Ocean Boulevard one of the most scenic roads in Palm Beach. Ocean front property owners have access to the beaches via a tunnel under the boulevard.

The first lake-side "mansion" in Palm Beach was built by a Denver financier, R.R. McCormick. Known as *Seagull Cottage,* it was purchased by Henry Flagler to serve as his residence until his mansion *Whitehall* was completed.

Whitehall is the white marble palace Flagler had built as a wedding gift for his third wife, Mary Lily.

Vivid yellow paint became known as *Flagler Yellow* for Flagler's fondness and extensive use of the color. It was used on The Royal Poinciana Hotel as well as on his private railroad car.

Diversified architecture helps to create the charming and elegant ambiance of Palm Beach along with tropical foliage, manicured lawns, palm tree lined streets, and roads decorated with symetrical floral arrangements.

The beautiful scarlet blooms of the Poinciana tree inspired Flagler to name his first Palm Beach hotel *The Royal Poinciana.* Indigenous to the island of Madagascar in Africa, the Poincianna tree flourishes in the West Indies and south Florida.

The tranquil and scenic lake trail was a popular path for a ride in a *Lazy-Back* during the late 1800's and early 1900's. Today it is a favorite with strollers, joggers, cyclists and sight-seers.

The splendid *Palm Beach Hotel* is an example of Mediterranean Revival architecture of the 1920's. Corinthean columns, Spanish bell towers, Moorish trefoil arches and simple wrought iron balustrades illustrate the mixing of styles.

The most dramatic part of *St. Edward's Catholic Church* is its Baroque entrance of double panelled doors and delicate stained glass windows. Land for the church was donated in 1926 by E.R. Bradley, the gambling casino owner who always chose to sit in pew no. 13.

The most sophisticated fire-fighting equipment is housed in an architectural landmark built in 1928.

The Brazilian Court Hotel still maintains its intimate elegance and relaxed atmosphere which helped to make it a legend in the 1930's. The hotel drew such hollywood greats as Errol Flynn, Cary Grant, Carol Channing and Gary Cooper.

The Colony Hotel, one of the smaller and more exclusive hotels in Palm Beach caters to the needs of the most discriminating clientele.

A classic example of the Mediterranean Revival style.

(Left)   The World Famous *Breakers Hotel* is a masterpiece of Italian Renaissance architecture. It was designed by the New York design firm responsible for the Waldorf-Astoria.

The hotel's main dining room retains its grandeur from a by-gone era. The more than 400 vintage wines in the cellar are sure to please the most discriminating wine connoisseurs.

The *Breaker's* lobby exemplifies genuine classic beauty. Fifteenth century Flemish tapestires adorn the walls, bronze and crystal chandeliers hang from the ceiling which was painted by seventy-five European artists.

The charming sunny courtyard at *Via Mizner* is a favorite spot for casual lunching.

Quaint retreats and tropical drinks make Palm Beach a favorite vacation spot.

Palm Beach offers a wide variety of dining possibilities from exclusive restaurants to casual European cafes.

Located within the confines of a lovely courtyard is a popular watering hole and eatery.

Mizner brightened his architectural works with colorful tiles and breathtaking bougainvillaea shrubs.

Mizner positioned his offices and residence overlooking fashionable *Worth Avenue*. Incorporated into the building are two shopping courtyards, *Via Mizner* and *Via Parigi*.

The flamboyant architect Addison Mizner could be seen during his time walking *The Avenue* with a macaw on his shoulder and several monkeys leading and following behind him. His favorite pet monkey, *Johnnie Brown,* was given an honorable resting place in Via Mizner courtyard.

Mizner named *Via Parigi* (Italian for Paris), in honor of Paris Singer. Singer made it possible for Mizner to unweild his architectural talents.

Distinctive shops tucked away in the charming vias have helped to build *Worth Avenue's* reputation for international excellence.

Whether it is window shopping or an all-out shopping spree, *Worth Avenue's* Esplanade has something for everyone.

Running the width of the island from the Atlantic Ocean to Lake Worth, *Worth Avenue* is lined with over 250 shops including residences and *The Everglades Club*.

Worth Avenue boasts an impressive list of exclusive boutiques, designer shops and specialty stores known worldwide. Cartier, Ungaro, Channel, Bonwit Teller and Saks Fifth Avenue are among the list of stores.

Worth Avenue now rivals Rodeo Drive as one of the most expensive shopping streets in the world.

Worth Avenue's beginning can be attributed to Paris Singer's foresight as well as Addison Mizner's unique architectural talents.

International fashions and Mediterranean architecture combine to make *Worth Avenue* a unique shopping street.

Contemporary art by Duane Hanson as well as collections of such masters as Monet, Renoir, Picasso, and Matisse are displayed in the numerous galleries and museums.

(Left) Beautiful fountains and statues are the center of attraction in picturesque vias and courtyards.

During the season, many fund-raising cocktail parties take place at the Gucci courtyard.

Whitehall's oppulence has been restored as *The Henry Morrison Flagler Museum* and is registered as an architectural landmark of national significance.

(Right)   The sixteen imposing columns that surround *Whitehall* were constructed from seven different varieties of marble.

Still part of Palm Beach's social life, Flagler's mansion is the scene of charitable events, concerts, ballet and opera productions, lectures and art exhibits.

Designed in 1938 by Maurice Fatio, *The Society of the Four Arts Library* was the town's first public library. Located behind it are meticulously manicured beds of roses and a Chinese garden with a lily pond which are attributed to the *Garden Club of Palm Beach*.

The library's entrance loggia is adorned with murals on canvas depicting the four arts: Art, Drama, Literature and Music.

Palm Beach abounds in cultural attractions. Ballet, dance, opera, symphony, theater and lectures are featured throughout the season.

Ballet Florida's world premiere of Vicente Nebrada's *Romeo and Juliet.*

Giuseppe Verdi's spectacular masterpiece *Aida,* presented by Palm Beach Opera and conducted by the internationally renowned Maestro, Anton Guadango, who has also conducted such greats as Luciano Pavarotti.

Nearly all of the world's 10-goal players, including Memo Gracida, compete at *Palm Beach Polo and Country Club* making it the "winter polo capital" of the world.

Polo originated in Persia in the first century as a training game for calvary units. Today most of the best polo ponies are bred in Argentina.

Palm Beach Polo becomes a royal affair with an occasional visit
by Prince Charles.

Over 150 golf courses and more than 1,100 tennis courts in Palm Beach County make this a golf and tennis enthusiast's paradise.

The perfectly manicured lush green croquet courts at *The Breakers* are a site for U.S.C.A. Championships.

A dock adjacent to *The Breakers* once served as a port of call for
oceanliners departing for Havana and Nassau, where Flagler
owned two hotels.

The ambience and distinctive service of the classic *Breakers Hotel* endures, luring long-time visitors back year after year.

Mizner's tribute to Palm Beach is *Memorial Park* in the center of County Road.

The impressive entrance to Palm Beach, *Royal Palm Way.*

A number of sea turtles can be watched as they use the beaches for nesting.

South Florida thunderstorms depart as quickly as they've come, bringing the much needed rainfall.

One spectacle that most visitors miss —just off the coast of Palm Beach — are the thriving reefs adorned by tropical fish and vividly colored coral.

The slender, leaning trunk of the coconut palm can reach heights of 25 meters (80 feet). Its coconut fruit is one of the most important crops of the tropics.

The blue Atlantic ocean and the serene Lake Worth offer endless sailing and boating possibilities, from windsurfers to million dollar yachts.

America's second largest tourney, *The Annual Arthur Smith Kingfish, Dolphin, and Wahoo Tournament* of *the Palm Beaches* attract hundreds of anglers.

On *Worth Avenue,* children may also purchase almost anything their little hearts desire. Whether *they* are spending a few dollars to hundreds of dollars.

Palm Beach residents enjoy boating throughout the season.

Although decades have past since Bradley's *Beach Club* was torn down, gambling enthusiasts can try their luck aboard a cruise ship departing daily from the Port of Palm Beach.

The wheat-like stalks of the sea oats which are common to the area's beaches help to stabilize shifting dunes that cause erosion.

Palm Beach, more than any other Florida city, has an ideal sunny
climate due to the geographic location of being closest to the
warm waters of the Gulf Stream.

"O 2B TAN" on a Palm Beach license plate. Tanning is always fashionable in the warm sunny climate of Florida.

The Annual Antique and Classic Car Parade offers a nostaligic look at past legends. From 1903 Daimler Benz to a 1936 Bentley Sedan. Parading down *Worth Avenue,* participants dress in authentic clothing of the period and later assemble at the *Flagler Museum.*

Different forms of transportation have taken the place of the *lazy-backs* of time past.

The Grand Prix of Palm Beach provides world class competition among the world's top drivers along with 700 horsepower and 200 mile per hour excitement.

Two of the closest finishes in IMSA Camel GT history were set at *The Grand Prix of Palm Beach.*